FORAGING FOR BEGINNERS

A PRACTICAL GUIDE TO FORAGING FOR SURVIVAL IN THE WILD

CRAIG JONES

Foraging for Beginners

A Practical Guide to Foraging for Survival in the Wild

Craig Jones

Disclaimer

The advice and strategies found within may not be suitable for every situation. This work is sold with the understanding that neither the author nor the publisher is held responsible for the results accrued from the advice in this book.

Content to Expect

SHIFT DIGITAL PUBLISHING
JOIN OUR COMMUNITY OF READERS
ENJOY PRIVILEDGE ACCESS TO PREMIUM CONTENT
Join Now

Introduction

Imagine yourself on an island far away from the comfort of your home and far removed from civilization. Imagine that you are there with your friends or your family and you are running out of food with no option to restock, what would you do?

When survival becomes the most critical thing in your life, you will wish you had some foraging skills beforehand rather than having to the dangerous approach of trial by error.

Foraging for survival is a beginner's guide for anyone who wants to learn how to forage but does not know-how. It is a very important guide to have on your side whether you are foraging for survival as a result of being exposed to danger in the wild or you are just foraging for fun.

One thing every aspiring forager has to know is that not all plants, animals, or mushrooms are safe to eat no matter how inviting they may look or how pleasing they are to the eyes. Some of these plants have been known to cause harm after a long time while some do not waste time at all in creating their negative effects.

You also have to be aware of possible allergies that you may have if you eat certain kinds of plants so that you do not unnecessarily endanger your life while trying to forage. As with other human endeavors, having the right knowledge is very important which is why this book was written with someone like you in mind.

In any case, this book is not all about gloom. It also has various sections that tell you why you should be foraging if you haven't already considered it or started. There are various compelling reasons why if you have not yet considered it, you would find foraging an interesting experience.

For those who also wonder how foraging came to be, you will find an interesting section that talks about that. You will also be introduced to some of the tools that can make your foraging experience a very interesting one. Having the right foraging equipment can sometimes be the difference between having a pleasant experience or a very nasty one, which is why a lot of effort was put into ensuring that you are shown the most basic tools and sometimes obvious equipment like a knife and other essential or sometimes nice to have foraging gears.

Unlike other books that only show you how to forage, where to forage, when to forage, benefits of foraging, safety precautions to know when foraging and foraging equipment you may need, this book will also show you the various ways you can store the various items you can successfully forage so that they remain fresh or edible for the time you want to consume them.

With this foraging guide, you can quickly get started and start foraging as soon as possible without harboring any more fear.

Chapter 1

Introduction to Foraging for Survival

To understand how survival interplays with foraging, we have to establish what foraging is first. It is in simple terms the hunting of wild food for consumption. Meanwhile, survival will be what all of us are hoping to accomplish—staying alive.

Therefore, foraging for survival is the hunting of wild plants for consumption as a means of sustenance to stay alive. This is as opposed to going to the supermarket to buy groceries. Even if it took an hour-long ride to get there or simply a walk around the block, it is still not going to be classified as foraging. Oh, don't forget going to the farmer's market, that's not foraging either.

Around us, trees, grasses, forests, and various plants exist. Surely our predecessors have narrowed that down to a few choices of leaves as herbs or salads. But out there, we still have many undiscovered edible plants. There are still greens hidden in the wild that are up for the taking. That's what a forager does–discover these undiscovered edible plants.

Imagine you're on a hike and lose your compass or can't find your way home. How will you survive? Of course, you may hunt for animals, but what if you have no tools for hunting and you do not know how to do that? What's your solution going to be? To forage. The trees and grasses won't skedaddle once they see you coming. So your best bet would be to survive on these until help comes or you decide to be Tarzan.

How Foraging Came To Be

Foraging is not a new fad that is being explored in movies just in case the world system collapses. No, it's been existing since the beginning of time. We can trace foraging back to the hunter-gatherer societies.

They were a nomadic society that moved as the seasons changed, eating whatever food they could find and allowing the wild to provide for them. They remained well-fed and healthy. What this means is that just because you're not eating the typical canned, prepackaged foods doesn't mean you won't be healthy. So don't be afraid to explore the wild.

Natural food is healthy and good for the body. but you'd need to know what to look out for, and that's what this book is about.

Benefits of Foraging

The forager's lifestyle is not an easy one, but it's immensely profitable. No one's going to ship the wild food to your doorstep but going out and getting these foods yourself can have many benefits.

Let's explore them.

i. Foraging is doubly beneficial because you're hiking and finding food at the same time. You're unwittingly exercising.

ii. Nothing saves cost like free food and the food of the wild is as free as it gets.

iii. It affords a connection with the world. We've built houses that have kept us in, and most people are reluctant to explore the natural world. They feel safer in cities. But going out of our comfort zone allows us to experience the world differently. We learn the unique workings of nature.

iv. Today, there are many theories about what causes illnesses. Processed foods have a giant question mark on them because of the processes that get them to that state. Imagine cutting out most of these, which will automatically increase your likelihood of remaining healthy for a long time.

v. The joy of discovery. Finding new things is fun. No wonder kids love to explore. It's about rediscovering that child-like wonder and using that to explore the world.

vi. Not only does foraging improve physical health, it also improves our mental health. Being around nature's green, breathing in fresh clean air is therapy.

vii. Without debate, foraged foods are highly nutritious and unaffected by processing like store-bought foods.

viii. Foraging can also lead to the discovery of different unique tasting foods and flavors that are undiscovered anywhere else.

ix. Assuming you get lost or stuck in the wild or the world ends and there are no more ready-made foods, the foragers and their kin may very well survive for longer. This skill can save your life and that of your family. Nature provides sustenance and you can find it.

x. Flowing from the point above, medicinal herbs exist in the wild like the burdock root. Knowing these beneficial roots and plants can save a life, if it ever comes to that.

Hazards of Foraging

Foraging may have many benefits, but dangers also exist. Some problems one may encounter are:

i. Poisoning oneself: This occurs when a person eats a poisonous plant or handles a toxic plant. Therefore, take extra care. Some poisonous plants can cause dizziness, nausea, seizures, and even death. So, though foraging may be fun, it is not a light affair.

ii. Destroying the environment: The excitement of foraging may make us forget that the environment thrives on the preservation of these wild plants. Stomping through the wild and destroying plants or harvesting more than necessary or taking the only plant in an area is essentially destroying the environment. Wild animals need some of these plants to survive more than we do. So, we should take care when foraging to carry only what is necessary and leave the rest for other foragers and wild animals.

iii. Going against the law: Foraging is a delightful activity but shouldn't contravene any laws. It's easy to trespass or forage on prohibited grounds if one is not careful. This can lead to an arrest or worse, a conviction. So, you need to be sure that where you're foraging is safe ground.

iv. Dealing with unusual foods: Depending on the person you are, this may be a welcome challenge. Others will steer clear of the unusual. Wild foods, as with all foods, have their preparation process, and this may involve days or weeks to get the product edible. Do not despair, patience is key when dealing with all things wild.

Chapter 2

Types of Equipment to Use for Foraging

Before you get all excited and start outdoors, let's talk about your foraging gear. What to wear, what to carry, what to use; we will extensively discuss these.

For our purposes, we'll divide these types of equipment into four kinds, protective gear for you, tools to assist you with harvesting plants, storage for different plants, and the miscellaneous.

Protective Gear for You

Wear Loose, Comfortable Clothing

When taking on a foraging mission, make sure you wear comfortable clothes. Comfortable means clothes that are easy to move around with, because you're going to do a lot of bending, stretching, and sometimes, kneeling. You'd want to wear clothes that don't inhibit your movement.

Long pants will protect your legs from insects and a long-sleeved shirt. And on days when the weather is colder, you can add layers of clothing to keep you insulated. A pair of socks too will prevent your feet from blistering when you have to take long walks.

Wear Boots

Nature's beautiful, but not tender. Boots protect your feet from thorns and sharp sticks. They're also essential in wet, swampy areas where you may have to trudge through mud, you definitely wouldn't want to dirty your feet. Boots will protect you from crawling insects like scorpions. They won't be able to chomp through your boots and get to your feet.

Wear a Wide Hat

In sunny areas, it's always advisable to carry a hat. All edible wild plants don't grow in the same area, so you may need to do a lot of walking to get to them. Nothing is more off-putting than the sun beating down your back when you're trying to concentrate, so get a hat.

Raincoat or Poncho

In rainy climates, it's advisable to wear a raincoat or poncho. Possibly, you may spend more time foraging than you initially projected, so you must be prepared just in case it rains.

Gloves

A pair of thick leather gloves will protect the hands while picking thorny plants or possibly poisonous leaves. Plants like nettles, blackberry stems, poison oak or ivy, and poison sumac are harmful to the bare skin. Gloves would protect the hands when handling these. Just wash your gloves properly after you handle any toxic plant.

First Aid Kit

In case you sustain a cut, a basic first aid kit can be handy for cleaning and dressing a wound until you can get the proper care.

Bug Spray

Bug spray is an insect repellent that you can apply on your skin or surfaces to discourage insects from perching. Using bug spray on your body should protect exposed parts from mosquitoes, ticks, and other creepy crawlies because they are many in the wild. You can reapply insect repellent, but do it after 6 hours or more.

Sunscreen

Of course, we can't leave out the sunscreen. As earlier pointed out, foraging is going to take a while in the sun and to protect your skin from the ill effects of the sun, apply some sunscreen.

Common Tools for Harvesting Plants

Although it is possible to forage plants with your hands, there are a few special tools that can make the process a lot easier especially when dealing with some roots and certain kinds of plants.

Foraging Guide

When going out to forage, a field guide is going to be an essential tool to be armed with. This is super important. You'd need to be sure that what you're picking is the right plant. Edible plants look similar to toxic ones, so you'd have to be completely certain before plucking them. They may grow side by side, so you must have a guide or more to direct you on what to pick. Make sure you get a guide that is specific to your region.

Knife

A knife is every foragers' essential. It can be a small knife for sniping off simple leafy greens or a chopping knife that can cut through dense, thicker roots.

Trowel/Shovel

A trowel or shovel can dig up roots. You can use a sharp stick, but it's always best to have your tools at hand. It saves you time, and you don't have to soil your hands by digging with your fingers.

Magnifying Glass

A magnifying glass will aid you in spotting the micro features of plants. There are things your eye won't pick up that would be important in determining whether a plant is edible, so a magnifying glass is very useful.

Clipper

A clipper, like a small knife, is an easy tool to use in sniping off tender leafy plants.

Scissors

You can use a pair of scissors in place of a clipper or small knife. It's handy and easy to use to cut off soft stems.

Brush

A vegetable brush can clean roots before packaging them. Just brush off the sand and have a cleaner root. Of course, you may use your gloved hands, but that's just more work and it will be better if you direct your energy to something profitable–like picking more plants.

Storage for Different Plants

Containers

It won't do to get your plants then have no place to put them. Having special containers is very important. For instance, berries can get squished if pressed so flat plastic Tupperware will work well.

Basket

A cute basket will work for the storage of roots like hickory, burdock root, and wild potatoes.

Sealable Bags

Sealable bags can be paper bags or any bag that allows air to seep through. A bag that is too tight or hot may kill green leaves in a short time. So an airy bag will allow the leaves to breathe and stay fresh.

Water

Heat dulls the color of leaves and weakens them so you can pour water into a plastic bag to keep the leaves fresh. You can also wash your hands and fruits before eating.

Others

Camera or a Smartphone

A camera to take shots of your wild edible plants or to do more research is important. You can also keep a documentary of the areas you have foraged for memory's sake or as a guide to go there again.

Notebook and Pencil

A notebook and pencil can jot down thoughts or views or discoveries of which you'll have many. So don't forget to take those.

Snack

You'd grow hungry and no, you can't eat the next green leaf you see. We can't let hunger lead you to eat something potentially harmful. Take snacks and plenty of water, foraging takes time.

Backpack

And, of course, you need a backpack to put in all your equipment.

So, this is a basic list. You may not need to take all the listed items, you should rather add some which are unique to your needs, just really be sure about what you want to accomplish on your forage and take the tools that'll help you do a good job.

Chapter 3

Factors Dealing with Foraging

Different factors affect a forager's ability to find and get wild plants. These factors include the location, the season, and the forager's experience.

First, plants grow where the topography supports their nature. Therefore, a plant that may grow comfortably in a rainy climate may not thrive in a dryer climate. So the location matters. Most people will assume that a forest will be abundant with edible plants, right? Wrong. A sunnier region with tons of rainfall will produce more fresh greens and edible plants than a thick, dark forest. This is because sunlight and rainfall on fertile earth is the recipe for bountiful produce, but a forest is dark, and sunshine doesn't reach the soil where edible plants can thrive.

However, this is not absolute. When in season, the forest can provide trees with fresh fruits and nuts for eating. So, understand that no matter how great the forager is, if the location does not provide edible plants, that forager won't find any. A forager cannot forage in a desert, the environment has to provide the plants for us to explore. Therefore, some plants you may find in the Northern hemisphere, you probably won't find in the South hemisphere.

Secondly, the season matters. The frozen winter does not support plant life. So, any forage expedition that you may carry on then will be for ice and snow. Except, you live in warmer or moderately cold regions that still allow plant life to persist.

Even then, it's not a walk in the park foraging in winter, so if you put on warm clothes and step into the woods, you may find edible evergreen conifer needles, redwood, pine, and hemlock which make great ingredients for tea. But be careful, the conifers of the yew tree are poisonous.

Other winter finds are berries, tree sap, tree barks you can infuse in drinks. Nuts and seeds like acorns, maple tree seeds, and dork seeds are also great winters finds. You can find certain leaves, flowers, roots, and mushrooms in winter. It may pose more work for a forager, but it's not impossible.

Best Season to Forage

Many will be presume spring to be rife with plants for picking, but these plants are new and still dense with water so they cannot provide sufficient nutrients and sustenance for a forager or their kin. As with all rules, there are exceptions. In early spring, new plant life sprouts, and most of these tender-looking plants are tender on the taste buds too. In a few months, the older plants may become bitter, so it's sometimes best to get them while they are young and fresh. Some of these plants are common like chickweed, dandelion, garlic mustard, and clover.

In the summer, fruits blossom everywhere. Berries like blueberries, wild strawberries, and elderberries are in full bloom. Milkweeds, joy-Pye weed, fox grape, chicory, and daylily are also available in the summer.

But by far the favorite season for foraging is autumn, especially the month of November. In autumn, there's an abundance of hazelnuts. Squirrels may get there first but no worries, you can always check under the leaves and in the hollow parts of the trees for nuts. Apples are also abundant in this period. You won't need to purchase them because they're everywhere around you, just waiting for you to pluck them. Blackberries are also plentiful. Make sure they're ripe before plucking so you don't get sour ones. They don't have a long shelf life, so you have to use them the same day or freeze them and store them.

You can also harvest cattails that grow in swampy areas. Wild grapes are also rife during autumn, but they look like Canada moonseeds which are dangerous so it's important to be careful and know for certain you're picking a wild grape and not its poisonous look-alike.

You can also get rosehips, persimmons, and sumac during this period. Wild onions and sassafras whose roots make great tea are significant finds for autumn too.

There are a plethora of plants, nuts, and fruits you can forage during autumn, so don your forager's hat and take on the great outdoors during this colorful season.

And third, your experience and expertise will determine how much you can forage. Drop a person who knows nothing about wild plants in the middle of a bounty and they won't know where to begin. That's the difference between a person who has no skill and an expert. Of course, no one starts out being an expert, but your determination to learn and practice will correlate with how well you'll do on the field. So, take out your guides, study and practice. Start with simpler plants so you don't poison yourself and give it up altogether. Foraging has long-term benefits, so think of it as a long-term skill. Go easy on yourself but don't give up. Practice, practice, and practice.

FT DIGITAL
PUBLISHING
JOIN OUR
COMMUNITY OF
READERS
ENJOY
PRIVILEDGE
ACCESS TO
PREMIUM
CONTENT
Join Now

Chapter 4

Where to Forage

In the previous chapter, we understood that location matters for foraging. Here, we'll dive into the forager's hotspots and the forager's not-spots!

A few choice locations to forage are:

i. Your Lawn: Yes, right outside your house. We often underestimate the value of what's right in front of us. Here's a tip; a real forager isn't the one trudging through the forest, it's the one finding wild plants and those plants could be right in front of you. If you're new to foraging, it's a great way to test yourself and hone your skill before taking on a larger terrain where you have to worry not only about plucking plants but also navigating your way, so you don't get lost. So, pick a magnifying glass, your trusty small knife, and a container and forage through your unmown lawn. It will surprise you with what you can find.

ii.   Your garden: If you're a gardener, then you must have dealt with pesky weeds. How about stopping for a minute, checking a guide book and finding out whether what you assumed was a weed is only really an edible wild plant that has been seeking your attention this whole time? Don't dismiss any plant until you know for sure.

iii. Local Parks: Most local parks have beautiful flowers and a rich undergrowth of wild plants. However, these parks may have laws that prohibit foraging in them. Enquire and know for sure. Even if you can't pick the wild plants, it'll be an excellent exercise to spot and get acquainted with them in a controlled environment. You can also volunteer to be a part of the maintenance crew and use that opportunity to pick your choice of edible plants.

iv. Private property: Know anyone who has a forest growing around them, and you'd just like to see what mother nature provides on those private grounds? I thought as much. But before you go skipping on their property and you're later charged, take permission. Always ask the owner of private property if you can forage on their land. Except they have something sinister going on, most will agree. So, always ask and don't trespass.

v. Swamps: When someone mentions the word swamp, it almost always triggers a negative reaction. What's good about a swamp? Well, foraging's good about a swamp. Maybe a swamp isn't great for farming, but some plants thrive in that location! Put on knee-high boots and take on that swampy land. You may find some raspberries, gooseberries, mushrooms, and blueberries.

vi. Marshes: Like swamps, marshes are wetlands. The difference between them is that while swamps are filled with trees, marshes have sparse trees. But marshes are covered in herbaceous plants such as hedges, reeds, and grasses. If you think this sounds like a forager's dream spot, you're right. In a marsh, you'll find plants such as pickerelweed, American elder, spatterdock, reed grass, watercress, cattail, and if you're lucky, some wild rice.

vii. Trail sides: Trail sides are perfect for picking different berries, leeks, mushrooms, and other edibles. Just keep an eye out for what you may find.

viii. The forest: Certainly, the first location that comes to mind when someone mentions foraging, and for good reason, the forest is the highest concentration of plant life. However, while you may imagine that the forest is crawling with wild edibles, this is a yes regarding fruits and nuts but not necessarily littler leafy plants. We may find these smaller plants in the forest but might not be as robust and as plentiful as those found in sunny areas because the tall trees block out the sun. You don't have to feel discouraged, your forest forager dreams are still very much alive. You can find burdock root, clovers, pennycress, amaranth and so much more.

ix. Edges of Farms: Like gardens, "weeds" litter the edge of farms, but you glue your forager eyes on that one plant you recognize as edible. And as with private property, if it isn't yours, take permission before picking off someone else's land.

x. Abandoned Buildings: These are not usual foraging spots but are a top spot for finding edible wild plants. And what's best is that if you live in a city with no way to find a forest or farmland, an abandoned building is excellent for that. Imagine no one has cleared the surrounding lawn in years. It must be rife with many plants to test your abilities and make new finds. So, the next time you drive by an old building, don't see how it doesn't fit into the rest of your city, see your new foraging ground.

xi. Riversides: This includes streams, creeks, and anywhere you can find fresh flowing water. It's not news that the banks of these water bodies are bursting with green life. So, these are indeed choice spots to find the water chestnuts which free flows on water, cattails, edible ferns, water lettuce, and so many more edibles.

xii. Hilly areas: Hilly regions also provide a great place to forage and discover new edibles. It will be an uphill climb, but a very profitable one if you know what to look out for. Get a trusted guide specific to your location and keep your eyes focused.

xiii. The coast: The coast offers not only a unique trove of plants, but we don't speak about them a lot. But, if you are vacationing or live by a sea or large body of water, foraging in rock pools and on the beach can carn you unique finds and also in the woods around the coast. You may find seaweed, dulse, wild leeks and dewberries, and even sea beet which is called sea spinach.

The places where you can get edible wild plants are anywhere there are wild plants. Do not limit your imagination. But explore the world around you.

Where not to Forage

As much as the world is a forager's playground, it's also other people's playground and these people may have protective laws or these areas may be dangerous for hiking and picking, just be certain you're not getting into trouble for the sake of wild edibles. Places to steer clear of are:

i. Someone's property where you do not have permission. We have already stated this, but in case it wasn't clear at first, this can be an offense, so avoid doing it.

ii. Plants growing by the roadside may look rich and lustrous, but they can be harmful to the health if not properly cleaned before eating. Fumes from vehicles or pesticides sprayed on them can make them unsafe. If you're uncertain about the edibility of a plant because of where it grows, it's best to leave it and go to a more natural environment.

iii. In public locations where there are specific rules against it. We create these rules to either protect endangered species of plants or preserve the composition of plants in that area. As a forager, don't ignore these laws. We love these plants and want to use them, but we also want to preserve them and not get into trouble.

iv. A person new to foraging must take care not to venture so far into an unfamiliar terrain that they can't get back out. If you're new to an area and would like to forage there, you can inform someone who knows the area to show you around or if that's not possible, scout the area first, keep markers and ensure you can get back out no matter how far you go. And you can also inform someone of your location so they'll know where to find you or use a compass. By all means, don't get lost in the wild.

v. Dangerous woods: Some woods are not only made up of green trees and hopping rabbits, there could be dangerous animals out there. So, before you explore an area, research what dangerous animals you may likely encounter. Ask locals, ask Google, and be safe. Foraging shouldn't be an extreme sport against nature.

Chapter 5

How to Harvest Plants

So far we've explored what tools to use when foraging, where to forage, but before we get into the type of plants to forage, how can you forage? This may seem basic, but many make the mistake of just pulling roots straight out of the ground or breaking off a branch. But foraging is an art and a forager must handle it with care for the sake of ourselves, the wild animals that also live on these wild plants, and for other foragers. Let's dive into how to forage.

The method used in harvesting plants largely depends on which part of the plant you're harvesting. Is it the flower, leaves, root, or stem? We harvest all parts differently, hence the many types of equipment we discussed in the earlier chapter. Now you'll learn how to use these instruments to harvest plants.

As mentioned, every part of the plant demands a unique method of harvest so we'll explore each individually.

Roots: To harvest a root, you must be certain that it's the one you want. You'd also need to be certain that it's not the only kind around the area which is to ensure that others who need it will also get it and it's not an endangered species.

The best way to get a root out of the soil is by using a shovel to dig a circle around the root. Most roots grow wide with branches extending out of the main stem, so you want to preserve every part. Dig around the edge of it and remove all the dirt between the root branches. A little bending down and getting in there with the hands to dig will do it. After that, you'd need to pull it out. That's why you want to free it of all the dirt, so it doesn't get stuck and break off.

Some plants may have deeper or wider roots, and others may be thinner. So depending on the plant, it may be harder to harvest. And also, the quality of soil is a factor, is the soil a thick, sticky clay or is it light sandy soil? Is the ground dry? Is it wet? These are relevant. It's important to know what you're dealing with so you can have all the tools ready.

Summed up, the process is to dig, remove dirt and pull.

Flowers: Flowers are the most delicate part of any plant, so take care when harvesting them.

If the flowers are small and grow in clusters, it'll be hard to pick them off individually. It is easier to snip off the stalk that carries the flowers and put them in a container, so you don't lose any.

For flowers that are bigger and have wider petals, picking off a flower will just involve holding the flower at the base and pulling it out.

Some flowers are even broader and a petal is equal to many smaller flowers. You may not need all of them, so what you can do is simply harvest an individual petal, a few, so the rest of the petals can ensure the plant lives on.

Leaves: Harvesting leaves is direct. Pluck off each leaf at the base or cut off a bunch. Tender leaves are best but are still usable when older, it may just be more bitter or less potent.

Other parts of plants to harvest are;

Tree sap by puncturing a hole in the tree and using a hose connected to a container to collect the sap. This may take a few days. But for pine trees, you can simply pick off the solidified sap at the spots where a branch breaks off.

While most fruits will fall on their own, the best and freshest are usually still high up. We can collect fruits by climbing up a tree and shaking the branches vigorously so the fruits fall. Or using a basket picker to reach up to the fruit and tug on it.

We collect nuts the same way by shaking the tree but ensure there are bowls or a cloth spread out over the floor to collect the nuts.

In collecting the different parts of plants, there's no best method. Follow what will benefit you most.

Chapter 6

Here, we'll be looking at the edible wild plants and those that a survivalist can live on. We'll also go through the toxic plants so you'll know what to avoid. And if you're stuck and can not consult the internet or you do not have a foraging guide with you, how you can detect whether a plant is edible. We'll discuss that in this chapter as well.

What to Forage

We can divide wild plants to forage into greens, mushrooms, roots, fruits, herbs, nuts, and seeds. Some plants may overlap, as many of their parts are useful.

Wild Greens

Wild greens are plants, which we call weeds, and are in our surroundings, in farms or gardens. Types of wild greens include:

i. Dandelion: The dandelion is arguably the most popular wild edible plant. It is not only common, but every part is edible. From the yellow flowers which contain lecithin to the roots that can make a special tea that improves the health of the liver.

It is great as a detoxifier and a diuretic because of its medicinal properties and bitter taste. It is also a digestive stimulant. The young dandelion that grows in a shaded area may be less bitter than a full-grown dandelion that grows in the sun. The edges of the leaves are shaped like a tooth and the leaves are smooth, unlike the false dandelion which is hairy. It grows close to the ground, unlike its look-alike that grows tall. Dandelions are rich in potassium, vitamin C, and iron.

ii. Amaranth: The amaranth plant which is also called pigweed is popular for its seed, but its leaves are also edible and are slightly sweet. You may find it in abandoned gardens around you. It can be eaten raw or cooked. For only a few calories, you can get nutrients such as iron, calcium, potassium, and protein.

iii. Nettle: Nettles, also called stinging nettles, can be recognized by their arrow-shaped leaves that have scalloped edges capable of stinging, if you're not wearing gloves. The root, stem, stalk, and seeds can be used for therapeutic purposes but it's the leaves that are mostly eaten. Unlike other plants that you can eat raw, nettles have to be processed because of the fine hairs on them. These hairs are the plant's protection against predators. It can be processed by steaming, drying, or preparing in a vinegar solution.

iv. Sorrel: Sorrels are of the buckwheat family. They are common in gardens and disturbed lands. The leaves are shaped like arrows and with reddish stems. It has a lemony or citrus-like tang depending on your taste buds, and you can include it in a salad. You may even forgo adding lemon to your salad because the sorrel already covers that. It is also great when paired with fish. You should only eat it in small quantities.

v.   Purslane: Purslane is available in cities and suburbs and you can even find them in cracks on the sidewalk. It's succulent and nutritious and you can eat it raw or cooked. The flowers, leaves, and stems are all edible. It can either be salty or taste like citrus. It is rich in vitamins, potassium, and several minerals.

vi.   Lamb's quarters: Lamb's quarters are a green leafy plant that look like spinach. They grow in temperate regions and are easily identifiable by their scalloped leaves and whitish underside. You can cook its leaves like spinach, and it gets a bitter taste when cooked. It's a rich source of vitamin C, A and K, potassium, and other minerals.

vii.   Chickweed: Chickweed is a soft green plant with five divided oval-shaped leaves. We can find it in wet and cool conditions where there isn't much sunlight. The stalk and leaves can be eaten raw or added to tea. Chickweeds are rich in chlorophyll and contain a healthy dose of vitamin C. It is also used for medicinal purposes.

viii.   Plantain: Wild plantain are of two kinds; broadleaf plantain and narrow leaf plantain. They are easily recognizable and grow close to nettles. The leaves can ease the sting of nettles. They commonly grow where the soil is moist and can be found in many gardens. Plantain leaves contain vitamin C and are rich in calcium.

ix.   Wild garlic: Wild garlic grows in woodlands and is recognizable by its broad, long leaves and potent smell. It's pretty easy to find. The leaves taste like a milder form of the common garlic and are a delicious addition to risotto, pasta, or mashed potatoes.

x.   Wild fennel: Fennel commonly grow close to rivers or along the coasts. All parts of it are edible but it's mostly the feathery leaves, the seeds, and bulbs that are commonly used. It is also use for flavoring meals and can make a delicious tea.

Mushrooms

Mushrooms are delicious fungal plants that can be added to meals. The texture is full and meaty and can give a dish an exotic feel and make home-cooked meals fancier.

Despite the allure of tasty mushrooms, the poisonous counterparts abound and are very dangerous. No, you won't only get diarrhea, it can kill. So even though foragers advocate for all other wild foods, mushrooms are treated with care. If you're a newbie, take along an expert when going to pick mushrooms. Assuming you don't know someone, take a trusted guide book or three. The point is, confirm beyond all doubt that the mushroom you're picking is not poisonous. Even after this, you can taste only a bit, wait a couple of days and confirm that it doesn't harm you before eating.

As with any plant, practice will make you better at spotting them. Common edible mushrooms are:

i. Chicken of the woods: Found in eastern North America, these mushrooms can be spotted where they grow in clusters on hardwood trees, especially oaks. They are large, flat, and bright orange. The texture is like chicken meat so it's great for soups and when sauteed. When old, it can be indigestible, so be certain they're young ones. Its poisonous counterpart grows on conifers and should be avoided by all means.

ii. Chanterelles: Chanterelles are large, shaped like flowers, and are gold. You can find them during autumn months in forest areas. Unlike Jack-o'-lanterns, their poisonous look alike, they're not clustered at the base. They grow singularly. You can enjoy their fruity aroma and delicious taste when sauteed and added to casseroles and soups.

iii. Morels: They are brown and shaped like a cone. They have a spongy look and one can easily spot them. Only, as all real edible mushrooms, they have poisonous look-alikes. Poisonous false morels are reddish, fat, and don't have the cone shape and the half-free morel which is longer than the edible morel. Morels have a rich flavor that chefs love, but as with all mushrooms, you need to know what you're doing before you pick them.

iv. King Boletes: This is the most common type of bolete mushrooms and is popular in Italian and French cuisine. It has a round flattish cap that is reddish-brown with a spongy underside that comes in different colors like yellow, white, orange, or red. It grows from summer to fall and you can find them under birch, hemlock, or aspen trees. You may eat it raw or cooked and used in sautés, soups, and stews.

v. Shaggy mane: The shaggy mane is large and easy to spot, which is great for beginners. It has a tall cap that is cylindrical and as it grows older; it turns reddish-brown and dry with flat scales on the sides. This mushroom has many gills that start from white and transform into black. It grows all over the U.S. from summer to early fall and during the winter months too. You can eat it raw or cooked.

vi. Chaga mushroom: Looks can deceive, and with Chaga mushrooms, this is true. This mushroom is neither colorful nor pretty. It may look like it's poisonous, but it's not. It is large and black, very hard and cracked. This part is considering the fruit of the fungi because the real mushroom grows underground and pushes this part out. The underground mushroom is inedible. Chaga mushroom is common around the U.S. and Canada, and if you get a taste for it, it grows all year round.

So there's a plus. The hard, black part is excellent for tea and you can use it for medicinal purposes.

vii. Maitake: Maitake also known as the hen of the woods is a huge mushroom that can weigh up to eighty pounds. It's called the hen of the woods because it grows in clusters that end up looking like a brown hen. It's difficult to spot, but when you do, the taste is well worth it. Its tough texture, delicious meaty, and smoky flavor are suitable for any mushroom dish.

viii. Oyster mushrooms: They grow like shelves up deciduous trees like aspens and willows all year round. Like the name, they are shaped like oysters. They have wavy edges and are white or ash in color. But their smell isn't pleasant. Don't let that deter you, they are tasty and can be eaten whole either raw or cooked.

ix. Puffballs: They are big and round and can resemble a golf ball or in rare cases, a soccer ball. It is white at the center and may have cracks when it matures. It turns yellow or brown as it ages. You can find it on lawns, parks, and in the woods during the summer months and early fall. Make certain the inside is bright white. If it's getting old and changing color, do not eat it. If there are caps, gills, or stems on it, then you do not have a puffball but a poisonous look-alike. You can sautée puffballs or use them to replace eggplants.

x. Beefsteak: Beefsteak mushroom looks like a beefsteak, hence its name. Younger ones are in fact pink on the inside and have red juice. It's common all over the US from late summer to early fall. The young ones are great when sauteed in butter, and the older ones are nice in soups and stews. It can even replace meat.

Roots

Roots can be a significant form of sustenance for a survivor because unlike leaves, it packs more calories. It also has medicinal benefits for one who doesn't have access to modern medicine. But to harvest roots, you have to be conversant with what the leaves look like to ensure you're harvesting the correct plant.

And while harvesting, keeping the stem and leaves intact allows you to be certain you've harvested the correct one and not the neighboring plant.

Types of edible wild roots are:

i. Burdock root: The leaves of a burdock plant are large, flat, heart-shaped, and have wavy edges. Burdock plant is common around the world and in North America too. It takes up to two years to mature. When it's matured, it develops a flowering stem. But, for the beneficial uses of the root, you'd need the plant that's still in its first year and does not have flowers. It possesses a long taproot that may be difficult to dig up, but when it comes out, it's worthwhile. It contains nutrients such as carbohydrates and protein. Burdock root not only has medicinal properties that can calm a fever but can act as a diuretic. You can eat it raw or cooked.

ii. Chicory: Chicory is a flowering plant. It's purple and has long thin stems. It grows under poor conditions so you can easily find it in urban areas, abandoned buildings, and on roadsides. The roots are bitter to eat raw but you can use them in place of coffee. It's rich in minerals and vitamins. Plus, it's easy to harvest and you can simply pull it out of the ground.

iii. Cattail: Cattails love to grow in wet, muddy areas and can be a significant find by riverbanks and creeks. Just be careful not to pick them from ponds or areas with polluted water because you may ingest harmful substances from the contaminated plants. Since cattails grow in regions with soft soil, they are easy to harvest. Loosen the soil around the plant before harvesting it. After it's harvested, it'll be dirty. Wash it properly before eating. You can eat it raw, but it's better when cooked because it's more easily digested.

iv. Daylilies: Daylilies are common, and you can find them easily in the summer because of their bright red flowers. They are very common and you can even spot them on the roadside. The roots taste best in autumn. They are great to eat boiled or raw, but only the young ones. The older ones are inedible.

v. Dandelion roots: Dandelions have long, reaching taproots. When harvesting, dig deep around the plant before pulling it out. Dandelion roots are edible all year round but are best in spring. You can simply prepare it by chopping it and boiling it, but you can also eat it raw.

Flowers

The petals of flowers are useful to add color and flavor to dishes, and others have medicinal properties. Wild edible flowers to forage for are:

i. Echinacea: Commonly known as purple coneflower, the echinacea is a flower recognized for its medical usefulness by the indigenous North Americans many years ago. The leaves of the plant are narrow and shaped like a lance and have scalloped edges. The flower resembles a daisy with its deep purple color. They blossom in summer until early fall. You may find them in gardens or wooded areas in the wild. The flowers and leaves are all edible.

ii. Violet: Violets are popular garden plants which are also known as garden violet, sweet violet, or common violet. The flower grows like roses and can either be deep violet or white. You can find them at the edges of the forest but they also do well in gardens. The sweet to sour taste of the petals makes it a great fit for a salad. It can make syrup and the leaves are also edible.

iii. Tulips: Tulips are beautiful flowers originally from North Africa, but now, they've grown around the world. In the wild, there are up to seventy-five variations of the flower. The leaves are bluish-green and the flowers are cup-like and shaped like stars. It grows around mountains and temperate regions. The petals are sweet and can enhance a meal. Do not eat it if you're allergic and never eat the bulb.

iv. Snapdragon: Snapdragons also called dragon flowers are called so because they look like a dragon's mouth. The leaves are shiny green and have a lance shape. The flowers come in various colors like white, bright pink, and red. They thrive in rocky areas. Unlike tulips, the snapdragon flower is not sweet but sometimes bitter or bland. We extract oils from the seed and dye from the flower. The leaves and flowers are anti-inflammatory and have been used to make poultices.

v. Garland Chrysanthemum: Garland chrysanthemum also known as Japanese-green is rich in minerals, vitamins, and antioxidants. The flower is daisy-like and is a mix of white and yellow. It grows in mild or slightly cold places, but if summer arrives; it turns into premature flowers. You can use the leaves in stews, soups, casseroles, and hotpots. While you can add the stem can to a stir-fry.

vi.   Daylily: Daylilies are fascinating flowers that only bloom for a day. They blossom in the morning, then by nightfall, they fall off only to be replaced by a new flower on the same stalk. Several species of daylilies grow in clusters. The long, linear leaves out to create arches and the thick roots store food and water. The flower itself possesses three petals and sepals that look similar. They are usually the same color, but they may also be different. Every flower has six stamens. Originally native to China, Japan and,d Korea, gardeners worldwide now grow this flower. They can adapt to any soil and temperature and can bloom twice in one season, but mostly in spring and sometimes during summer and autumn. The young leaves of some species are edible, but the flowers are great additions in soups.

vii.   Chives: Chives are like onions. They are available in stores and grown in gardens. Rich in vitamins, iron, and calcium, they also repel bugs and attract bees, which is good for a garden. The flowers are a pale purple, shaped like stars with six petals in clusters on top of the stem. They bloom during spring in the south and early summer in the north. Chives thrive under the full, bright sun, and in colder temperatures, they shrink back into their buds to resurface in spring. We use the stalks for added seasoning in meals because of their onion-like flavor. The flowers can decorate dishes and the stems are used with fish, potatoes, and soups.

viii. Red Clover: Red clover doesn't last long and is great at attracting bumblebees. The leaves come in three and are green. The flowers are dark pink and grow pale at the base. They are a significant addition to herbal tea. However, excessive consumption may cause side effects like rashes, nausea, and aches.

ix. Hollyhock: The hollyhock is a beautiful flower with dark petals. Its leaves are soft and dappled, shaped like that of wild oak. It has large flowers which are pink, yellow or orange. It can grow in clay soils or sandy soils. The flowers have medicinal value and can serve as a mouthwash for bleeding gums and anti-inflammatory purposes.

x. Dianthus: The dianthus flower is also called pinks, carnation, and sweet William. The leaves are grey or blue-green. The flowers have five petals that are pale pink or darker. However, a certain species has yellow flowers with a purple center. The flowers have a spicy flavor.

Fruits

Fruits are delicious, don't require cooking, and are a great starting point for beginners. They're a complete meal and contain lots of vitamins. There are many fruits in the wild and some of them are.:

i. Wild apples: Wild apples are like domestically grown apples. The major difference is that the wild fruits may be smaller and the growth less even. However, it's still very delicious and great for making cider because of its slightly tangy flavor that domesticated apples don't have. Crab apples are tiny, some even as small as peas, and you can make jellies with them.

ii. Black chokeberry: Black chokeberry also called Aronia berry is recognized as a superfood. It tastes like red wine and a cross between sweet and bitter. They may be red or black, but most people argue that the black ones taste better.

iii. Autumn olives: They are considered an invasive species because they grow everywhere, even on the roadside. No condition deters autumn olives. It has tiny fruits that may be round or oblong. They are sweet and succulent and are eaten fresh or made into jam.

iv.   Blackberry: Blackberries can be found in the summer and are easy to spot, which is great for new foragers. If there's any doubt, the thorny brambles give it away. They look like dewberries, which isn't a problem because dewberries are also edible. They can be used for wine and jam.

v.   Black Cherry: Wild black cherries are sweet fruits but getting them is the challenge. They grow on tall trees and plucking them before the birds get to them is highly unlikely. But in the south, on very large cherry trees, the cluster of fruits falls before birds can get to them so you can pick them up. The bark of the tree is used for herbal cough syrup. But the process is quite tricky. If the bark is not dried immediately it's harvested, it can ferment and become toxic.

vi.   Bunchberry: Bunchberries are majorly sweet. Beyond that, there's no other flavor. Their texture can discourage one because it's like mucus, and in earlier times people used it as a thickener for jam. They grow low and in tightly packed clusters, which make them easy to harvest.

vii.   Cranberry: Cranberries are commonly known for being a dressing, but they are wild fruits you can forage. They are easy to grow and grow well in wet soil. They freeze in snow and can be picked after the snow melts in early spring. It still keeps its sweetness.

viii.   Currants: These are tasty berries that are domesticated but can also be found in the wild. They are versatile and can grow in any condition. Blackcurrants are the most common type. But there are red, white, and pink currants too.

ix.   Wild grapes: Wild grapes are like domestic ones and therefore easy to spot. They may be tinier and not as sweet, but they can be exceptional for making jellies and wine.

Nuts and Seeds

Nuts and seeds are packed with calories and great for a survivalist. A 146g cup of peanuts can contain up to 828 calories. When you are surviving on wild food, this is a complete meal. They're also nutritious, containing much-needed carbohydrates and essential minerals.

These are a few nuts and seeds you may find in the wild:

i. Pine nuts: Most pines produce nuts, but not all are edible. The edible ones are from stone pine, pinon pine, sugar pine, digger pine, and ponderosa pine. During autumn, the cones of the tree will fall open and the large seeds will be exposed. These can be plucked and shelled by hand. You can eat some pine nuts, raw or cooked.

ii. Butternuts: Butternuts are tasty and very nutritious, having up to 3000 calories per pound. They spoil quickly so you have to use them up fast. They can be eaten raw, roasted, or baked.

iii. Hickory nuts: These are easy to crack but with the use of a hammer or another tool. Some hickory trees produce bitter nuts and they are difficult to tell apart from those with tasty nuts. Hickory trees with delicious nuts are the shagbark hickory, the shellbark hickory, and the mockernut hickory.

iv. Black walnut: Black walnuts are well-loved for their delicious nutmeat not only by foragers but wild animals as well. The difficulty is getting to the meat inside. It's very hard to crack so if you're foraging for black walnuts, carry along a hammer. Or you can peel off the husk with a knife until the meat is exposed. However, there's a brown juice within the husk that stains everything it catches so you can put on gloves before removing the shells.

v. Beechnuts: Beechnuts are highly proteinous and tasty. It's no wonder squirrels and raccoons love it. The beech tree produces casings every year but produces the nuts every three years. So, if you're foraging for these nuts, be on the lookout. They spoil quickly so after you harvest them, dry them under the sun or in an oven.

vi. Acorns: Acorns are common and rich in carbohydrates and proteins. But the bitter taste when raw is often a turnoff for many people, so if you have some acorns, the best way to enjoy them is to boil them in water for fifteen minutes, pour fresh water and boil it again. Repeat the process until the water is clear. This is to remove the component causing the acorn to be bitter and make it enjoyable.

vii. Pecans: Pecans are delicious nuts that are cultivated and sold commercially. They're a type of hickory nuts, but unlike the others, they're easy to shell. The wild pecan is smaller than the domesticated one but still as delicious. There are no known poisonous variations of it.

viii. Fennel: Fennel seeds are green and shaped like rice. They have a pleasant aroma that gives meals a delicious flavor. They also contain anethole, which helps to relieve constipation by soothing the muscles in the stomach. You can grind them and add them to tea or meals as a flavoring.

ix.   Poppy: Poppy seeds are tiny, round, and black and are gotten from the opium poppy. They are rich in antioxidants and can improve the heart's health. They also relieve body pain.

Herbs

Wild edibles may fill your belly but can't exactly heal you if you get ill. However, the wild also provides herbs that work just as well as modern medicine. Before the pharmaceutical industry, in North American history and all over the world, wild herbs were used to cure illnesses. Some of these herbs are still incorporated in supplements today.

These herbs are useful to cure stomach upset, fever, purify the blood, combat inflammation and many ailments. If ever you're without modern medicine, knowing these herbs and how to use them may just save your life.

Some wild herbs are:

i. Sunflower: Sunflower petals can be harvested, dried, and used to create oils for soothing wounds and swellings.

ii. Burdock root: Burdock is a great root for the liver. It also helps to calm down a fever. Even though it's very bitter, its medicinal benefits are worth it.

iii. Chicory: Chicory is similar to a dandelion in its qualities, it helps that liver too. The best time to harvest them is in fall, so mark the plants in spring or summer and harvest in autumn.

iv. Rosehip: Rosehips are the fruit of a rose plant. They can be red or pink and are slightly oval. They have a ton of nutrients including vitamin C. They make a delicious addition to tea and in soups or they can be infused in oils and used on the skin. Not only do they have lots of benefits, but the aromatic scent is also a bonus.

v.   Ginger and turmeric: Ginger and turmeric have so many benefits and are already well known. They are great in meals but also good for the health.

vi.   Mallow: The marshmallow root is great for curing coughs, acid reflux, stomach upsets, and colds. Its plant is identifiable by white flowers with a pink bud and lush green leaves that have rough edges.

vii.   Cherry Bark: The bark of the chokecherry tree can cure coughs and allow a person to sleep peacefully.

viii.   Dandelion: Like burdock root, the dandelion root supports the health of the liver. It aids digestion and studies have shown that it helps against cancer. It's a little bitter. The roots can be roasted and made into a coffee replacement.

ix.   Yellow dock: Yellow dock's roots and fruits can be used as medicine. It can cure pain and swelling in the nose and throat, heal skin diseases, and stop bleeding. The benefits of yellow dock are many.

x.   Plantain: The leaves of this wild plant can be crushed and rubbed on wounds, bee stings, and bug bites. It soothes the area and helps the wound to heal.

Other wild herbs include rosemary, wild garlic, coriander, chamomile, juniper, spruce, tansy, yarrow, chives, water mint, ground elder, ground ivy and so many more.

If you're interested in knowing more about wild herbs and using them, it's best to read about each of them extensively to know their uses and how to use them.

To use it for treatment, speak to your doctor and get professional recommendations.

Chapter 7

Safety Foraging Precautions

Most wild edibles have inedible and most times fatally toxic lookalikes. It is paramount that a survivalist knows what these plants are and how to avoid them. Being able to spot an inedible plant has already made your job easier.

These inedible plants are many, but there are common attributes that can be found in them and they are:

i.   Avoid plants with thorns

ii.   Stay away from flowers shaped like umbrellas

iii.   Mushrooms are too risky, if you cannot properly identify them, leave them.

iv.   If you see a plant with milk or discolored sap, avoid it.

v.   Avoid plants with beans or seeds in a pod.

vi.   Avoid plants that have an almond smell.

vii.   Plants with leaves that grow on trees are dangerous, stay away from them.

viii.   If a leaf tastes soapy or bitter, spit it out and rinse your mouth.

ix.   Stay away from plants that have shiny leaves.

x.   Plants with yellow or white berries are dangerous.

xi.   Avoid wild carrots because the inedible ones are toxic and are not easily distinguishable from the edible ones.

Some inedible wild plants to watch out for are:

i.   All the inedible mushrooms: This is probably the foremost wild plant that comes with a giant stop sign for beginner foragers. If you're not sure, avoid mushrooms because the inedible ones are deadly.

ii.   Harlequin Glorybower: The seeds of this plant are poisonous when eaten and touching it may cause a skin rash. It produces bright blueberries during the fall.

iii.   Mexican Poppy: These flowers are common in winter. Either white or yellow, they possess spiky leaves. Though not good for eating, they're used for herbs.

iv.   Tahitian Bridal Veil: This flower is not only harmful to humans but also dogs and cats too. It produces a white flower that look like the edible spiderwort plant.

v.   Spreading Lupine: This plant can be found in the south of the U.S. and spotted by its blue flowers. Though it's beautiful for decoration, the seeds are poisonous.

vi.   Wavyleaf Basket Grass: This plant is harmful to humans but not animals and is common in the south.

vii.   Mistletoe: This viny flower evergreen with its white berries has become synonymous with Christmas.

However, eating any part of it can cause a myriad of symptoms like nausea, dizziness, and even seizures.

viii. Horse Nettle: These are plants with green fruit that ripen to red or yellow. There are three types, and each has different times when they get toxic. The best thing is to avoid them always.

ix. Castor Bean: Castor bean produces castor oil. Though the oil is useful, the seed contains ricin, which is a deadly poison. A small taste of it can kill an adult who doesn't get treated in a short time.

x. Waxy or Glossy Privet: The Chinese have used this plant as medicine, but the seeds are a little toxic and other parts of it too, should be avoided.

This is not a comprehensive list of poisonous plants to avoid. It's just to reiterate that foraging is not all fun and sunshine and a forager should guard well against mistaking poisonous plants for edible ones.

Chapter 8

Universal Edibility Test

What do you do when you don't have a guidebook and can't check if a plant is edible? What if your life depends on getting wild food?

This is where the universal edibility test comes in. The universal edibility test is used to determine if a plant is safe to eat. You shouldn't eyeball a plant and throw it into your mouth at once. As we have seen, dangerous plants may look yummy, and most times, resemble edible plants. So what you should do is carry out a test to check if that plant is safe before ingesting.

This test follows a series of steps, and they will be laid out here. They are:

i.   Divide the plant: First, what you want to do is get a plant and separate it into different parts. Sometimes, some parts of a plant ate edible while the others are not. So, divide the plant into bud, flowers, leaves, stem, and root. If it doesn't have flowers or buds, then those don't matter. Make sure it's a common plant around the area so after you do the test and if it turns out the plant is edible, you can have more of it. What you do now is choose the part of the plant you want to test. Make sure you're doing this on an empty stomach. If you're in a survival situation, likely, you don't have food, anyway. But you may drink water.

ii. Skin contact: Next, you want to test it on your skin. If it's dangerous for your skin, then it's most likely bad for your stomach. What you do is take the part of the plant you're testing, for example, the leaves. Crush it and rub it on your inner elbow for fifteen minutes, then leave it there for eight hours. If it burns, tingles or you see a rash, rinse off the area and forget about that part. But if the area is fine, you may move on to the next step.

iii. Cook: Toxicity of plants may be reduced or eliminated after cooking so if you have access to a fire, cook that plant or if you don't and want to eat it raw, the next step can determine further whether the plant is safe. After you boil the plant or if you're eating it raw, take the part and hold it against your lips. If you feel a burning or tingling sensation, anything unusual, discard it and start with another plant part. If not, move on to the next stage.

iv. Taste it: Put the part in your mouth and hold it for fifteen minutes. If you feel any burning or tingling, spit it out and rinse your mouth. If it not, you can continue.

v. Chew: By now, if there's no adverse reaction, you can chew the part in your mouth thoroughly and hold it for another fifteen minutes. If there's a negative reaction, spit it out and rinse your mouth. If not, forge on.

vi. Swallow: After chewing and holding, you can swallow the plant. Eat nothing else for another eight hours, but you can drink water. If you experience nausea, induce vomiting, and drink lots of water.

vii. Ready to eat: If after swallowing and waiting for eight hours you do not experience nausea, then the plant is good for eating. Get a small portion, nothing much, and eat it the way you prepared it.

This is a long process, but it is well worth it if you can get food for many days. While you're conducting the test, distract yourself with other activities like fetching water, gathering wood, and making your shelter.

Chapter 9

How to Store Foraged Food

Ideally, foraged plants should be eaten fresh. But where you need these foods to cover for a period, you won't have access to them for example winter months or where you can't go out and get them, knowing how to store them will extend their shelf life and allow you to enjoy them for longer.

Some ways to store foraged plants are freezing, drying, canning, and fermentation.

Freezing

Freezing involves using extreme cold to keep a plant in the state in which you got it. It stops the growth of organisms that can spoil the food. The freezing should be done immediately after you get the plant, so it's still very fresh. Some plants might require blanching before freezing. This is docking the leaves in boiling water for a short time, then putting them in cold water to prevent them from cooking.

To freeze wild plants, rinse them thoroughly to get off dust or sand, then chop them into smaller pieces. Put the chopped pieces in an ice tray with clean water and freeze. After these plants are frozen in the ice, take out the ice cubes and seal them in plastic containers or airtight plastic bags.

When thawed, you can use it in soup and stew, but it won't be nice for salads. After you thaw it, don't refreeze it.

Fruits last when frozen and their texture, color, nutrients, and flavor stay the same. Fruits that can be frozen are pawpaws, persimmons, blueberries, blackberries, and elderberries. It's good practice to remove the seeds out of fruits that have them before freezing, so it won't be an issue after it's thawed and used.

Nuts and seeds last best when frozen. No need to remove their shells, you can simply bag them and put them in the freezer. Where there isn't enough space, you can remove their shells.

Drying

Drying a plant is an old and convenient method of preservation. Drying can preserve a plant for up to a year. When you want to use the dried plant, you can simply soak it inside water for some minutes until it softens.

Different ways to dry plants are:

i.   Air Drying

If the leaves are dirty, rinse them lightly and remove dead leaves. Then shake them out. If they're not dirty, no need to dip them in water.

Make small bundles of them and band them together with a rubber band. Using pegs, hang them to dry in an airy room. Plants with long stems are easy to dry this way. Simply band the stems together and hang. Don't dry them under the sun, that'll just turn them crispy and unusable.

Evening primrose seeds, peppergrass, amaranths, goldenrods, and mints can all be dried this way.

ii.	Sun Drying

Sun-drying foods like roots are a good way to preserve them. Simply get a box and open up the top. Slice the foods you'd like to dry into it and keep them in the sun. Using a box is good because you can easily take it in at night and return it out the next day until the foods are crisp and well dried.

iii.	Dehydrators

If you have a dehydrator, it's an excellent way to dry leaves. It maintains the nutrients that can be lost when dried under the sun. The leaves will also keep their rich green color.

Dehydrators can also dry berries, but you'd need to turn the berries constantly to make sure all sides are well dried.

After drying, you can turn your crisp leaves into powdered form by grinding or using a dry blender, then packaging it in a container and dating it so you'll know when they'll go bad.

Some plants do not retain their nutrients after drying, so research each plant individually to know the best method for preserving them.

Canning

Canning is a process whereby processed food is stored in sterilized jars. This is good for storing some vegetables, jams or jellies. There are varied methods to can food, but the aim is to preserve the food for a long period. To can food, sterilize the jar and lid thoroughly. Bacteria getting into the jar can spoil the food. Sterilize the jars and lids by pouring boiled water over them and allowing them to stay for a few minutes before using.

The acidity of the food will determine how long the canned food will be preserved. Foods with higher acidity last longer. If the acidity levels of food are not high, consider adding lemon juice, citric acid, or vinegar to increase the acidity.

Fermentation

Fermentation is a process whereby sugar and yeast interact to form alcohol. This form of preservation is good for fruits. Many wild fruits have yeast and sugar, so the process naturally occurs with them. A softening fruit, like persimmon, is already starting the fermentation process.

Though carrying out this process may need a more in-depth knowledge of fermentation, and special tools, it can simply be carried out by adding yeast to fruits and allowing the process to occur.

Where flies contaminate the wine-making process, the mixture may end up becoming vinegar.

Both wine and vinegar are useful and a good way to use and preserve fruits.

Other ways to utilize excess foraged fruits or berries is to make them into jam, jelly, syrup, or fruit butter.

Chapter 10

Safety Tips When Foraging

A forager's intuition is as good as the instructions he's given. While you're foraging, you may get an instinct about what to avoid, go with it. It's better to leave an edible plant as a form of precaution than to pick a poisonous plant.

In earlier chapters, a few safety tips have been dropped here and there, but in case you didn't catch them or we left any essentials out, we'd go over them one more time.

i. If you're going on a forage to the deep woods, protect yourself with the right clothing and pest repellent.

ii. If possible don't go into the deep woods if you're uncertain what is out there. Predatory animals may end up posing a greater problem than whether a mushroom is edible or not.

iii. Some wild plants can be eaten raw and others need to be prepared. Ensure you follow the rightful procedure of preparation, so you do not harm yourself.

iv. Take your guidebooks along with you or a foraging expert if you're starting out and even more when you think you know what you're doing.

v. Again, if you do not know what it is, do not eat it. If the tree you know normally bears fruit in the summer and you see this tree that looks a lot like the one you suspect it to be is bearing fruit in winter, then it's most likely a look-alike and may be dangerous. Expect your plants to have their usual behavior.

vi. Do not "taste" just to see. Except you're doing the edibility test. Don't take that gamble.

vii. Don't pick plants from polluted surroundings.

viii. As an act of goodwill, planting seeds of the plant you've foraged will help the environment produce more.

These are only a few safety tips, but certainly, as you progress and gain more knowledge and experience, you'd know what's good for you and what's not.

Conclusion

Foraging is not a common activity nowadays. Civilization kicked it out the backdoor as part of the old ways. However, it's a skill that is regaining its relevance because people need to learn to stop depending on established systems. What if these systems crashed? What if farmers and companies decide to stop food production? It's highly unlikely, but in case of any unexpected occurrences, knowing how to fend for oneself with nature's resources will be a lifesaver.

More than that, understanding food and what goes into our bodies is paramount. Foraging opens one's mind up to all the culinary possibilities and how these choices affect the body and health.

This book is the first step toward foraging, but a great one. Other books are specially geared to all the points discussed within these pages and will aid your foraging journey.

SHIFT DIGITAL
PUBLISHING
JOIN OUR
COMMUNITY OF
READERS
ENJOY
PRIVILEDGE
ACCESS TO
PREMIUM
CONTENT
Join Now